THERE IS A HOUSE

—— ✣ ——

Ruth Carr

SUMMER PALACE PRESS

First published in 1999 by

Summer Palace Press
Cladnageeragh, Kilbeg, Kilcar, County Donegal, Ireland

with the assistance of
The Arts Council of Northern Ireland

Printed by Nicholson & Bass Ltd.

A catalogue record for this book is available
from the British Library

ISBN 0 9535912 04

for
Tom and Beryl

Acknowledgments

Some of the poems in this book have previously appeared in:

The Belfast Review; Brangle; The Canadian Journal of Irish Studies; A Crazy Knot; Cyphers; Elle; The Female Line (Belfast 1985); *Fortnight; Gown; HU; I Know a Woman* (Belfast 1997); *Ireland's Women* (Dublin 1994); *The Irish Review; Krino; Living Landscapes; Map-Makers' Colours* (Montreal 1988); *New Orleans Review; North; Poetry Ireland Review; Sleeping with Monsters* (Dublin 1990); *The Ulster Tatler; Women's News; Women's Works* (Wexford 1992); *Word of Mouth* (Belfast 1996) and *Writing Women.*

Some poems have also been broadcast by BBC Radio Ulster and the World Service.

Biographical Note
Ruth Carr, formerly Hooley, was born in Belfast in 1953. Many of her poems have appeared in anthologies and journals. In 1986 her Revue was staged in Belfast and Cookstown, and a Monologue, *What the Eye Doesn't See* was commissioned and performed by Point Fields Theatre Company in Belfast and Glasgow. A member of the Word of Mouth poetry collective, she works as a tutor in adult education and has assisted various writing groups in publishing their own work. She edited *The Female Line*, the first anthology of poetry and fiction by Northern Irish women writers, and is currently associate editor of *HU* poetry magazine.

CONTENTS

Family Snap

This is the daddy in a disguise
unknown in a suit but the same limpid eyes.
Overtime pays for coats and shoes
bread he wins and tales they lose.

This is the brother in Sunday best
who stands up tall like a knight on a quest.
Leaving behind his imaginary friend
he wears a school tie and stares straight at the lens.

This is the sister in home-made dress
with turned-in toes and matchstick legs.
Her feet face the front but her body swings round
watching a shadow creep over the ground.

This is the holiday out of the sun
caught in a bright spell by the one
uniting three figures who shyly stand
hand in unfamiliar hand.

Boxed In

Each within the next
reveals a chamber
packed with secrets.

Field flowers
plucked and pressed,
only a breath of summer
left.
Every one I open
smells of you.

My Mother's House

You, descending the staircase
with a mewing black cat in your wake,
coming to the door with wet hands
or into the room with a tray of porcelain cups.

The day you went away
curtains hung unopened, rooms
held their breath, lost without
you to let in the light.

It grew too tall for you in the end,
cobwebs mocking you
and your bright, attentive ways
to make us all important.

I lived there, later.
Your house shuttered within mine.
Each time I wanted it to be you in the mirror,
watching, without white hair.

Finding a way to house the past
I see you better, back to the light
and when you visit me
it will be always summer in a shady room –

I will not need to ask.

Mother Love
for Joan Newmann[1]

without the words
I knew what everything was for
bed, sink, hearth, toilet, table

I hid in the warm, dark
linen smell of the hot press
where words and looks could not come in

felt my self
safe and secret –
drinking in darkness

my mother wrapped me
in the blanket of care
handed down to her

I poke my fingers through the holes
but can't get rid of it
the pattern a transfer on my skin

she muttered things like *Can't keep house
the way she did, look at the dirt of the windows,
the nets yellow with pipe smoke* . . .

all the while playing house with me
tea parties under the table
divining out of scraps, designer costumes

for my teenage Jeanie doll
the one she chose
for me

drowned me in too big, too long
handmade frocks, lace-ups that picked me
out in party games

but I liked best on my own
to dress up in the clothes she never wore
flame red petticoat, full twirly skirt, peep-toe

shoes and hat with sweeping brim
sat, dressed to kill, impervious
to my brother's sidelong stare

we stuffed ourselves
with all her gorgeous
teeth-defying treats:

apple charlotte, upside-
down cake, queen of puds
treacle tart

and my father's favourite
apple-pie with cloves that you could bite on –
a salve for the ache.

The Touch of Words

Talking to himself replaces her
in the chair by the window where
he used to find her, staring at nothing particular
and picking a smile out of thin air
as she turned to see him pausing in the doorway
for a word – the empty chair
replaces her in timeless conversations
told by heart too many times
to leave the silence bare.

You Can Live On

You can live on in a house
that echoes their names.
You just don't enter those rooms,
draw the curtains, close the doors
quietly, do not disturb.
It asks too much of you
to feel your way round
the warm-to-the-touch, worn,
familiar back of her favourite chair
or to finger the fruitless bars
of a clean-stripped cot.
It asks too much.
But you can live on in a house
that echoes their names.

Feeling Small

One of your hands
conducting absent strings
catches hold of mine
by your side at last.

Where have you been?
Child-wide eyes search me
for answers which do not come.
You resort to orders –
Get my cap, my shoes, let's be gone . . .

Back to the man
who could make things work
who carried the wounded
the drunk, the undone,
who could walk . . .

Back to your mother
hands on her hips
filling the doorway with waiting
for you to come home.

Your other hand
no longer owned, a dead loss
weighted on your heart –
Toss it in the sea,
feed the gulls with it.

Time to leave
and you beg me
to take you with me
plead for just one sweet.

I hold you in arms
not big enough to hold you
feel the child that I am
leaving you adrift
too far out to come in.

One last look
we play soldiers and salute
pretend
we are not deserting each other.

The Lost Child

Still there
with no sound but the bleat of a heart
I feel more than hear your bird-hunger
bird-mouth open wide, bird-fingers
inside the nest in the tree in the picture
shading my bed.

Still there
between me and the other 'mummy, mummy' ones
limpet limbs clamped to my ribs
limpet cries catching my breath
I find you and lose you again
to your flat little body.

Still forming
the word both of us deny
both ache to be said
still waiting to be called by name
oh, stillborn child of my ingrowing, grafted self
I am still bearing you.

Nursery Rhyme

M is for mummy
and man that I saw
out through the window
bare toes on the floor.

The man in the moon
winked back when I waved
but mummy came in
and shushed him away.

She curtained the window
and tucked me in bed
but I hear him tapping
inside my head.

M is for mummy
and man that I saw
out through the window
bare toes on the floor.

Childcare

When our son cries out
from the depth of night
for the demons besieging
his mind and small, sleeping body,
it's his father who hears,
is first to his side
remembering.

Waiting for Rain

The simmering volcano in the kitchen
scorches the tips of a child's tendril fingers.

A well of fire rises to seep through fissures
that furrow like nerves along brittle terrain.

I bear the name mother carved on my heart-land
where cattle still graze as ash coats their backs.

A memory of rainfall beats in dry places
where smoke is stifling the lark in its path.

I open the door and imagine a cloudburst
I touch my own earth and remember the dance.

We Share the Same Skin
for my mother

We shared the same skin, your touch
home to my body. To grow up
I built walls, defining
where you ended and I began.

It was a child sulking to shut
you out. You waited, a quiet
stream for me to surface in.
That's where to find you now –

hunkered down on a river bank
needle or pencil in hand, sometimes
pins in your mouth, sometimes humming,
or leant against some stubborn

wind-spent tree. You showed me that
obvious thing – that under the skin
there's human, that dressing up is
a game fit only for children.

That obvious thing that nobody does –
you did it most times,
shared your skin with so many,
I needed to know you loved

me more than any old refugee.
I walled up inside, let my body
go begging for crumbs like poor Tom,
a craving that couldn't find centre.

But we shared the same skin
and when yours grew too tired
and too yellow to care –
with a child of my own but still

not grown up, I couldn't let go
until prodigal waters burst
mortar from brick, I broke through
to your salt-bedded river.

We share the same skin, my daughter
and me. She's building walls
to define where I end
and she can make a beginning.

Red Riding Hood's Mother

I am cleaning my daughter's shoes last thing at night
the house to myself as I gently press
my fingers into the toe of no glass slipper –
these days Dr Marten's the fitting shoe
for a young girl's foot.

I am watching the polish glide on with the guilt
rubbing what isn't a kindness into the heel,
only this far can I go –
wax melting on contact, proofing the steps
of one whose feet I would dress
in anemones from the wood.

Turtle
for Kate

I

Born within the safe sea wall of shell,
you break out and make for the great, wide water.
Ungainly on land, you instantly glide and swoop
to the heart of the ocean, at home on her bed.
Turtle and woman, we share more than dreams
which draw me, like you, to the surface for breath.
You carry me, come calm or rough water,
through all thirteen moons on your back,
waxing and waning in time with the tide
that closes the circle on each of our lives.
Wherever I go, in graceful or slow motion,
there are walls to break through and water calling me back.

II

It's not what you do after
but before the egg cracks that counts.
The strong, deep strokes that steer
your cargo clear of teeth-rimmed doors.
The heaving strokes that drag your laden body
on to land in the full of the moon.
You dig until the sand and water meet
amicably – a damp, cool, comfortable womb
to lay your unborn babies in,
beginning their life on earth with a burial.
It's your thick-skinned turtleness I admire
would like to wear as mother.

The Gift

I will not wipe the stickiness away
stuck with runny nose and something sweet
the press of small lips planted lightly on my cheek
your gift of plum-juiced kiss will stay

with me throughout the hours that we will spend apart:
me in endless meetings, bottle-necks,
you meeting other children, all learning the steps
of give and take, how to suppress their heart-

felt tantrums like we do in suited meetings
dressing what we feel in thin disguise –
so civilised that I am glad to touch my cheek
and feel the imprint of your lips' repeating
lesson circled there. All our lives
this simple seal of love is what we seek.

Exile

Out here
in the eye of the storm
needle-threading is
art and survival.

By the sheltering glow
of your fire,
I can't even see
needle's eye.

We stab more than stitch
in rhyme more than rhythm
and nothing is sewn
into one.

Sinking sun
runs rivers of gold from my eyes,
my child born under a blanket
of stars in a seamless sky.

On Ice

You splashed about in the bath
with our daughter,
I neglected to scrub your back
and made dishwashing sounds
in the kitchen.

You left
silently
a watermark of love on her brow;

I pulled the plug
and watched our bitter-sweet waters
gurgle away,
not even a tidemark
of what had once been warm and moving.

Just one giant
glacial field
of porcelain white.

Resting Place

Manless to bed
she bares her body's every seam,
spreads her limbs across the bliss
of sheet-white emptiness,
stretched like poles along a tent
to house this jealous space between the breasts.
Drawing in the threadwork of her life
she lets them go –
the lean nomadic thoughts that press and press,
to wander through the nightscape
for a home.

Remnant

The smell of you that I carry
fragile as the moth on my old winter coat.

The smell that disintegrates
at the mildest inquiry into the state of us.

The smell that I quarry
in the recess of remembered places

the cave of your arms
the cup of your palm
the nape of your mythical neck.

The smell of you that cuts me adrift
on cedarwood and water
uncontainable as the sea.

Clearing the Table

I want to be restored
like an old oak table,
sanded down so every scrape
and ring-spill is scoured out,
down to the wooden grain of me
laid bare.

No covering to smooth away my age
I want the very lines exposed to light
that you may trace along my length
a nakedness, solid and able
for your hands, a written sheet –
a laden table.

Cup with a Crack

I drink from a cracked cup
which used to be white.
Now no amount of water will wash out
the stain of years ingrained
with too much taste.
It will not be replaced
until the crack grows more than I can bear,
or by some accident it breaks,
empties my last drop across the floor.

Giant Clam

Indispensable as air, a vague appendage,
member of myself crammed full of facts like
Einstein's relativity and when we last held hands.

But if I drop below the surface
wet my elbows fishing for a clue,
my memory snaps shut, a tight-lipped clam.

And when the water shifts, displaced
by some big fish or falling tide,
it leaves me like a turtle on dry land.

I spend my idle moments, head under brine,
combing the ocean floor with forked limbs
divining nursery rhymes.

The Spider in the Bath

Like the broken pencil
or the empty glass
my bath remains undrawn
because of you.

One moonlit night
I'll dip myself in ink
and watch you spin.

Watch the pattern grow
and know how delicate
the thread that I could break.

That you would simply
cast your life-line out
and start again.

I will begin.
Trace from memory-skin
my own unwinding line
of make-believe.

Outside Your Door

A human voice,
moving over water
falling air
standing stones.
You are there
to listen to the rain
beat scribbled rhythms in your ear,
to reap the wind
and store its giant strength
in stone-work houses built to last.
I shelter there,
crouched among the rocks and cotton grass,
in company of those the stones bear witness to.
I brush against their shapes
and feel them stare.
For you are there before me –
you make shadows on the page
creep down the hill,
I chase them still across your land.
Time after time
I stumble on their footprints in my mind
to find myself again
outside your door.

Anatomy of an Artist

This gentleman has compiled a particular treatise of anatomy . . . and of whatever can be reasoned about in the bodies both of men and women, in a way that has never yet been done by any other man.
Antonio de Beatis, 1517

The ringed bird tilts
lop-sided into the blue.
Trailing her quill
in the scientist's ink
she plots the impossible journey
of fall and spring.

Da Vinci sought a similar curve
dissecting every sinew in the wing
to reach where skylarks sing. For every Icarus
the downward flight begins.
Only in two dimensions
under the sun

did he spread unerring wings
divining the instinct
that leans on the wind,
that transfuses everything.
He returned all the parts to the thing itself
the vessel to its dreams.

Woodblock with Wren

for Kerry Hardie

You lift
out of wood
water, webbed with light
dancing dark and bright
with earth-born secrets.

You lift
out of water
bird that hides, the wren
merging and emerging
set for flight.

You lift
out of bird
song in the veins and grain
of wood, water, wren –
the beating wing.

I lift
out of song
memory, desire to touch
the wood, water, wren in me –
my own resin.

In Hokkaido

In Hokkaido
the Japanese crane
in long black stockings and feather boa
picks her way through dancing snow
now you see her
now you don't.

Symbol of happiness
perched on stilts
like tentative thoughts of summer
she persists
where bears are baited in concrete pits
in Hokkaido.

Corncrake

She sits on –
maybe slow-witted, maybe brave
as the locust machine grows black.

Earth shuddering beneath the shell
beneath the rim of her body
threatening to crack.

Air chokes
corroding lungs
the steering hand could crush.

She sits on
in a shrinking world
that cannot hold the jarring of her note.

Straw bales out behind, a neat-bound
box for feathers, blood, bone
and untried voice.

He lasts longer
solitary
sounding out a harsh lament

for all their flightless futures
laid in a nest
our future won't accommodate.

Bird
that will not build above the corn
casually reaped.

Blue Edge

In the porch of my house
the tiles meet and part like lovers
at arm's length in dance.
Triangles melt into diamonds, squares, stars:
ivory, teak, terracotta, slate blue,
unremarked by the passage of feet.
Their saraband synchronised but for that one
blue partner turned the wrong way,
picking out mine from all porches.

I smile to myself in the cooling bath
warmed by that out-of-place tile,
gracing my threshold with human error
the beauty of imperfection.
I feel its edge breaking the pattern.

A Gift of Ox-eye Daisies
for Louise

They are still here,
kindly ones standing their ground.
Over a month since your call spilled blood orange
along my narrow field, the way the sun does
sometimes, moments before it goes.

Here, right through the difficult spring,
warming the empty fireplace,
every petal stained by human hand,
an ox-eyed herd of curious heads
stock-still, staring like children.

Although they'll fall away in time
their flowering on my retina will go on,
the burnt orange rim of your deeper sphere
an after-image opening my eye
to your survival.

Perennial as your words,
encoded freight from childhood,
your gift a difficult growing
beyond the dark
seeding my fallow field with helianths.

Parity

men lead lives of quiet desperation

H. D. Thoreau

In this land
where the law is like a public bar
with no toilet –
the men pissing out the back yard –
women lead lives
of even quieter desperation.

Our Lady

Our Lady, dispossessed
on some alpine ice-cap
would not look out of place
in ski-pants, zipping
down virgin slopes
to the sound of music.

But wait for her second
coming round the mountain –
the icon-shattering thaw.
Our immaculate image, white-iced
and frosted for two thousand years,
might melt to nothing more divine
than a seething woman, cheated
out of sex and a son in his prime.

Body Politic
for Anna

After you tore me, there was a clearing
still as the moment of stillness after words,

like coming upon a green space between trees
out of the undertow of roots and creeper and growth in darkness
face, limbs, feet, purpling, peeled raw.

Like this: your remarkable note
rising to meet the blue above our heads,

far beyond the clinical ceiling of this partitioned room
beyond the unsolicited stab of pethidine in my thigh
beyond the refusal to deliver you into my arms
beyond blocked roads and minds,

you came out
of my body
to claim your own

your voice breaking over every fixed thing

bearing me on its tide.

Your Blue Norwegian Cap
for Stephen

Your blue Norwegian cap
brimful with figures dancing,
a hat for trekking through snow.
Bells vibrate to the rhythm of deer,
their steaming breath that hangs like thoughts
we don't have language for,
soft and imprecise against the blue.

Instead I push you in your buggy to the bus.
We wait and watch clouds gather overhead.
You point to everything, traffic, dogs,
graffiti – all of equal moment to your eye.
And when it comes I haul the buggy up
the angled step and then stop short –
I feel his shadow falling every time.
Is this the seat he sat in, on his mission,
staring out the window, maybe humming
to himself, stroking the loaded gun that rests
so easy on his knee in the plastic bag?
Or is he one behind, his breath on my neck
curdling with mine? I sense him everywhere –
*Our hero, Rambo Stone. Next time you go
to Milltown take a tank . . .*

I pull your cap down tight
around your ears. Let's pretend
that we are somewhere far,
you in your red-painted sleigh
me a dark-eyed doe
that has not smelt the lust of dogs
bearing you away.

Community Relation
for Amy

Who is this urgent, longed-for creature
tugging the milk from my body,
who dreamed nine months in my inner sea
tumbling, kicking, hiccuping
while cease-fires were declared
in the world that she will absorb
like litmus paper?

Who can tell when the cord will be cut?
Wounds heal?
When recognition will blossom in a smile?
What the first new-coined words
of a common tongue might be?

To gather a child up to your shoulder,
cheek to your cheek,
is to hazard the perilous gift of love
into a no-man's land.

Along the Red Road

I come to a place
in the palm of my hand
where the road runs out
and there is nothing but rock.

Only my fingers,
wrapped around the need
to pass through walls
inside the heart
can find an opening,
let the stone roll.

No messiah,
white-skinned, red or black
can lift me up from Wounded Knee.
I hold or I release my own Drumcree.

Stepping into Lough Melvin

Creasing and smoothing
creasing and smoothing
the silver and dark of shot silk
seaming this shore to that.

Breeze that is a kiss off the water
sun an arm around my shoulders
tree that has grown all these years
for a body to lean against.

Black figures in a black boat
half-way in, half-way out
lines cast in blindness, to the very heart
of things that have no nice return.

In the here and now of it
I want to believe
that they can see right to the bottom,
as clearly as I see these stones

at my feet, formed of colour
not line, of themselves
enduring: drowned steps
waiting for lower waters.

But I know that boat, those figures,
that they will be with me whatever –
holding back, holding out, holding on
for the rising fish that never comes.

Let my eye draw me all the way out,
to dive right under without a line,
refract in a rainbow all I know
about love, about correspondence.

Hanging Tree

In the featherless heart of a night plucked bare
I hear what the crows have been calling
for hundreds of years;
I hear with an unstopped ear:
Caught in the tree, caught in the tree,
tongue of a woman with healing spells,
calling the wind, calling the moon,
calling on me to peck her free.

Like the Tree
in memory of Frances Farmer

Instead of cutting
out her tongue, they drilled a hole
in her cranium.

Her mind dismembered
like the tree, lopped for symmetry
to thicken wilful limbs
before they spread beyond the wall
or tapped the shuttered window
after dark;

completely cut off –
like the tree – Frances Farmer
still whispers in the breeze:
No performance once they pull the switch,
no words
that aren't already vetted in the script.

Mushroom

I am rinsing milk white mushrooms
under the tap. Your mouth opens birdlike
to gulp all the world it can,

incautious and whole.
A sliver of white in all that pink –
the first tooth is through.

A girl's voice on the airwaves
shocked by the hole
where her sister's cheek should be,

she can see right through to the teeth.
Thousands of splinters mosaic her child form,
this is the nuclear act embedded in flesh.

When she dies, her mother begs
Bury me with her.
Please, bury me with her.

I am watching skin peel like paint
plants recoil into themselves
seeking their own shadow.

Dust blooms with each step
as this wave burns us up,
but not to ashes.

Fifty years on
a girl's voice on the airwaves
fragments everything.

On the blank white space that is a mushroom
I visualise a mushroom field at dawn.
I drop one and it's gone.

Sukina

She smiles so sweetly from the photograph.
Headlines next to *Thatcher No Lame Duck*
and *Dubcek's Human Face.*

She wouldn't spell her name right, five years bold.
Daddy's savage lesson with a rule
and plastic tubing and his fists –

and still to come the kettle flex and plug.
He tipped her in the bath, he slapped her back
with salt, he beat her to a pulp.

She died of pain
and shock
and sheer exhaustion.

Daddy No Lame Duck
Sukina's Human Face
Tomorrow someone else will take her place.

Missing

Four feet tall
of stocky build
dirty fair.

No mention of her fears
her favourite colour, what her
dreams are made of.
Not a word of how she looks
at things but never sees the strings.

Out late at night, waiting for the light
I feel but do not feel the pinprick
rain, the other side of glass.
See but do not see
the disappearing back of some young girl
who could be four feet tall, of any build
hair drenched of all its light.

Find, under a dry roof
my children wrapped in sleep.
Even my woman daughter's head
staining the pillowcase
blue and cherry red.

May she find walls that are not unkind
somewhere that feels like home should feel
to lay her farewell head.

Story Line

In memory of Ann Lovett and her sister

Once upon an evening after school
This young girl, neither ugly nor beautiful,
Slipped past the Church
To squat inside a grotto on the floor.
Hugging a bundle of baby clothes,
She laid them out beneath the Blessed Virgin's chiselled feet
Before she bore a child with no man's name.
Unlike that ancient tale of starlit stall
No creature shared her secret or her pain
And only when her body broke with shock
Someone stumbled on them in the dark.

Her father racing with blankets for them both,
Placing the stillborn child between hot bottles all too late.
Carried to a car and then indoors,
She bled beside a weak, oil-burning stove
And slipped away once more without a word –
This time for good.
And everybody said *We didn't know.*

Backs closed around the grave, tight-knit in grief.
New-formed and full-grown child
Are lowered with all eyes and loss of face –
Spread across a million breakfast tables.
No excuse,
Nothing to be salvaged but a heap of little clothes
Which will not go to waste.

Lyn

You seemed to know things I just couldn't fathom,
with your bra and your visitor,
the dark-haired smile Da Vinci might have caught,
fluent at twelve in a way that left me
speechless, long after you'd gone.

Impervious to school, its grades and taunts,
you moved like a star in her firmament.
And when neither your sun nor your moon rose again,
orphaned, you went on, sure of the ground
as it opened beneath your feet.

Up on the train from Dublin, you
joked about the grim Masonic Home
that took you in. Still smiling, defiant,
you told me, *No need to worry, whatever they do*
I'll never eat horse-meat, I swear it –

our sacred pact when we were ten.

Sister

in memory of Frances Molloy

Like the hat on a high shelf
no longer new but tenderly kept
brimful with previous airings
and dreaming of the next,
you were the sister I dreamed of
who would always return
when the leaves turned black
or the teeth of a winter cracked
leaving gaps in the landscape.

Bareheaded, under an old moon
I open your touchstone book.
Words fan out like feathers
that wing through my skull.
Slowly, the silken spill of your voice
is washing me downriver
into a rimless sea.
Your Indian hat
comes floating back to me.

Jennifer

No seasonable going, you went
beyond recognition – one morning
from sweet-pea summer to winter blight,
a hedgeful of fuschia clipped back
to a pool on the ground.
No part of their dying down, falling red
and amber, interleave this autumn
with your name – beating through the hillside's
trampled grain, bleeding across the path of the setting sun
and breaking from the heart of the harvest moon
as only unimagined silence can.

Every autumn will remember you
in rosehip and in thorn
the blackberry's bruising blue
in yellow leaves lying on the ground.

Vera Matuskeva

Vera Matuskeva
you survived six years
of concentrated crime against your skin,
aged a lifetime.

Vera Matuskeva
you do not take
the taste of water not contaminated
the smell of air not laced with gas
the quality of light not filtered through flayed skin
without remembering.

Vera Matuskeva
you do not take a step
without your ungrown, unfed son,
sister, brother, husband and the one
you knew too briefly
and too forcibly to name.

Vera Matuskeva
I do not know the weight of it
the relics you unwrap
a tooth, a twist of baby hair, a ring,
a scrap of cloth so rubbed no pattern left,

the length of cord you also keep
in case it gets too hard
remembering
Vera Matuskeva.

There is a House
for Georgie

there is a house
whose door will not close in my face
where there is always a place for one more
at the table.

there is a house
that lets in light all the year round
even in winter the weakest of suns
reaches in.

there is a house
with walls that hold me like branches
with a roof of summer leaves
and roots that go deep.

there is a house
where I can be long and not outstay my welcome
where I can be low and not have to pretend
where I can be loved without trying.

for the house whispers
take off your shoes, rest your bones
here is room for your dreams
let me rock you to sleep

you are home, little one.

The Blue Bowl
for Peter

A go-between,
a traveller between hands,
a sacred proof of the journey
from me to you.
Caught in the cusp of china blue seas
we are waltzing on water,
embraced in this bowl
that opens its heart
like a miracle,
we carry and do not spill.